The Black Stone

A Five-Act Play

To watch the play, please scan the following QR Code:
The Black Stone

Dr. Sultan bin Muhammad Al-Qasimi

The Black Stone

A Five-Act Play

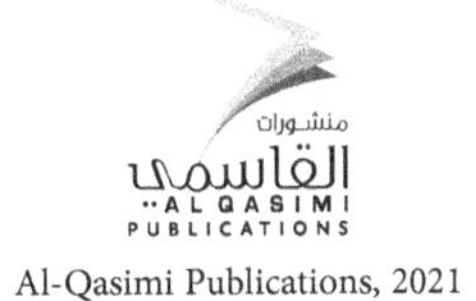

Al-Qasimi Publications, 2021

The Black Stone A Five-Act Play
First published in 2012 in Arabic as "Al-Hajar Al-'Aswad"
by: Al-Qasimi Publications
Author: Dr. Sultan bin Muhammad Al-Qasimi (United Arab Emirates)
Publisher Name: Al-Qasimi Publications
Sharjah, United Arab Emirates
Edition: First
Year of publication: 2021
© All rights reserved:
Al-Qasimi publications
Sharjah, United Arab Emirates

Translated from the Arabic by: Dr. Ahmed Ali

ISBN: 978-9948-469-52-0
Printing Permission: National Media Council, Abu Dhabi, UAE
No. MC 01-03-5671549, Date: 05-08-2021

Age Classification: E
The age group that matches the content of the books was classified according
to the age classification issued by the National Council for Media

----

Al- Qasimi Publications, Al Tarfa, Sheikh Mohammed Bin Zayed Road
PO Box 64009 Sharjah, United Arab Emirates
Tel: 0097165090000, Fax: 0097165520070
Email: info@aqp.ae

CONTENTS

Introduction

Muslim societies are currently witnessing many religious, social and political reforms. It is only when the enemies of Islam start to interfere in their affairs through directing extremists against such reforms that the reforms are branded as acts of terrorism.

In this play, The Black Stone, we are introduced to one of the ways of how the enemies of Islam interfere in manipulating the efforts of a good, well-intentioned Islamic movement and converting it to a terrorist movement.

The historical events dealt with here took place during the long struggle between the Abbasid Caliphate and the Qaramatians. The names of the characters and places including the dates are all true.

It is hoped that this play would provide the reader and the viewer with better understanding regarding the source(s) of terrorism, and that when one calls to the way of Allah that this Qur'anic teaching is adhered to:

"Call all to the way of your Lord with wisdom and beautiful exhortation, and reason with them in the most kindly manner". (Qur'an, AN-Nahl 16:125)

The Author.

Cast of Characters

- Caller (1)

- Al-Sayyida, *Mother of Caliph al-Muqtadir*

- Thumal, *Lady-in-waiting to al-Sayyida*

- Al-Muqtadir ibn al-Mu'tadid, *Abbasid Caliph*

- Gharib al-Khal

- Abullah ibn al-Mu'taz

- Mu'nis al-Khadim, *Abbasid Army General*

- Mu'nis al-Khazin, *Abbasid Court Treasurer*

- Nasr, *The Hajib*

- Junior Servant

- Voices

- Second Servant

- Muhammad ibn Da'ud, *Visir*
- Ali ibn Eissa, *Chief of the Diwans*
- Ahmad ibn Da'ud, *Judge*
- Yumn, *Hajib of Abdullah ibn al-Mu'taz*
- Ali ibn Muhammad ibn al-Furat, *Next Vizir*
- Saqlabi, *A Slav Servant*
- Junior Servant
- Voices (2)
- Abu Sa'id al-Jannabi (Hassan Bahram)
- The Commanders, *A group of 5 commanders*
- Guards
- Courtiers
- Sa'id, *Eldest son of Abu Sa'id al-Jannabi, the Qaramatian*
- Sulaiman (Abu Taher), *Youngest son of Abu Sa'id al-Jannabi*
- Arabian Bedouin
- The *Aarada* band
- Caller (2)
- Muhammad Sanbar ibn al-Hassan ibn Muhammad Sanbar
- Isfahan Merchant
- Local Guide

- Abul-Fadl Zakariyya, *A Son of a Persian King from Isfahan*
- Voices of a group of army men (singing)
- The entourage of Abu Taher, the Qaramatians
- Servant
- Furjah, *Mother of Sa'id and Sulaiman*
- Voices of pilgrims praying and supplicating
- A man introducing the Governor of Mecca
- Governor of Mecca

The Opening

Kinetic and expressionist formations to the sound of music. Devices representing the scientific progress achieved in the early Abbasid Caliphate (132 AH/750 CE – 279 AH/892 CE).

Act I

Place:

The Caliphate Headquarters, Residence of Caliph al-Muqtadir ibn al-Mu'tadid

Setting:

A grand hall with luxurious furniture

A voice calling from outside accompanied with drum sounds.

Caller:

O, people of Baghdad! Let it be known to all, present or absent, that on this day the 20th of Rabi'al-Awwal 296 AH, that Abullah ibn al-Mu'taz is now your Caliph. O, people of Baghdad! Let it be known to all, present or absent, that the Chiefs, Judges and dignitaries have all given *bai'ah*[1] to Caliph

---

1- Bai'ah is a pledge of allegiance, loyalty and acceptance as Caliph.

Abullah ibn al-Mu'taz. O, people of Baghdad! Let it be known to all, present or absent, that this day Muhammad ibn Da'ud is the appointed *Vizir*,[1] Ali ibn Eissa is the Chief of the *Diwans*,[2] and Ahmad ibn Da'ud is the Supreme Judge. O, people of Baghdad! Let it be known to all. Those present should inform those who are not …

As the calls are made, enters al-Sayyida, mother of al-Muqtadir. Her appearance, clothes and walk inspire awe. She looks worried and concerned as if she is expecting an important event. She looks one time from the window and another at the entrance door. With every new call she hears, she places her hands on her ears so that she does hear the caller. When the calls disappear, she looks up and raises her arms in supplication.

Al-Sayyida:

O, my Lord! I pray to you. You are the One capable of all things. Have mercy upon us. O, my Lord. My son is very young. He is barely 13 years of age. My Lord! He has not been a Caliph three months and since then we have been afflicted with hardships, one after the other. My Lord! His young aching heart cannot take it!

1- Visir or Wazir was then the highest-ranking official in the State, acting as the Caliph's aide and adviser, and under him would the Chief of the Diwans (Government Agencies) similar to Prime Minister today.
2- See note above on visir/wazir.

Knocking on the door is heard.

Al-Sayyida *(shouting for her maids)*:

Qahramana Thumal, … Qahramana Thumal.

Thumal:

Yes, my Lady

Al-Sayyida:

Check who's at the door.

Thumal goes then returns with a wide smile on her face.

Thumal:

My Lady! My Lady! Nasr, the *Hajib*,[1] says Abullah ibn al-Mu'taz has fled.

Al-Sayyida:

al-Hamdu-Lilah! al-Hamdu-Lilah! (May Allah be praised).

Al-Sayyida *(addressing Thumal)*:

Thumal, hurry up and get your Master, Caliph al-Muqtadir, out of his hiding place.

Al-Sayyida walks about in the hall until Caliph al-Muqtadir is brought in.

1- Hajib is the person who announces the Caliph's visitors before they enter the court.

Thumal enters leading young Caliph al-Muqtadir who is being dragged like a feather in the wind.

Thumal:

My Lady! The Caliph is here.

Al-Sayyida:

My son! My son!

She takes him by hand and they both sit on the couch. She pats his shoulders and fixes his garment, saying:

Al-Sayyida:

It has been two whole days since I last saw you! May Ali ibn al-Mu'taz be cursed!

Al-Muqtadir:

Mother, what happened?

Al-Sayyida:

This morning Abullah ibn al-Mu'taz sent for you commanding that you leave to the residence of Ibn Taher so that he is able to move to the Caliphate Residence. I acted without your knowledge and instructed Mu'nis al-Khadim, Mu'nis al-Khazin, Gharib al-Khal, our courtiers and followers to go and fight Abullah ibn al-Mu'taz.

Loud knocks on the door. Thumal rushes to check. She then returns and says:

Thumal:

My Lord! Nasr, the *Hajib*, says Gharib al-Khal is at the door.

Al-Muqtadir:

Let him in.

Al-Sayyida:

What happened? Why did he come back?

Gharib al-Khal enters holding his sword. His clothes have traces of blood and are torn in places as a result of a battle fight. He is panting, saying:

Gharib al-Khal:

We headed from here to al-Mukhram where Ibn al-Mu'taz was. There, we fought against his guards. He managed to escape with his *Vizir*, Muhammad ibn Da'ud, his Judge, Ahmad ibn Da'ud, and his *Hajib*, Yumn. But he is currently being chased everywhere by our courtiers led by Mu'nis al-Khadim and Mu'nis al-Khazin.

Gharib al-Khal:

My Lord! Chaos has spread all over Baghdad, and

there have been acts of looting and killing. Ali ibn Muhammad ibn al-Furat has taken it upon himself to restore peace and calm.

Al-Sayyida:

Gharib, please go and bring us Ali ibn Muhammad ibn al-Furat.

Al-Muqtadir:

Mother, what do you want Ali ibn Muhammad ibn al-Furat for?

Al-Sayyida:

He would be the best person to act as your *Vizir*.

Voices are heard outside. Nasr al-Hajib enters, shouting:

Nasr al-Hajib:

Ibn al-Mu'taz! Ibn al-Mu'taz!

He points at the door where he had just come in. All look in fear and shock.

Abdullah ibn al-Mu'taz enters, an old man, showing traces of battle fighting. His hands are tied with ropes and he is being pulled by Mu'nis al-Khadim and Mu'nis al-Khazin.

Al-Sayyida *(mocking ibn al-Mu'taz)*:

Wasn't the money you took enough for you?

Abullah ibn al-Mu'taz *(To al-Sayyida)*:

Since the murder of my father, Caliph al-Mu'taz, the State has been in decline. Our victories have turned to defeats everywhere at the hands of the Qaramatians. Instead of engaging your son with learning and attainment of knowledge and progress, you indulged him in satisfying his whims and desires. The whole State is now run by women and servants.

Could anyone believe that you appointed Tuman, the maid, as Chief of the *Diwan* of Justice?

You managed to ruin everything!

The Treasury has been bankrupted because of your actions!

The Muslims are divided because of you!

Al-Sayyida:

Was it us who killed your father, al-Mu'taz? No. It was his own Turkic soldiers who did it. And now, when you are in my house, and in my grasp, you dare accuse me of this nonsense?

Al-Sayyida *(talking to Mu'nis al-Khadim)*:

Mu'nis, kill him.

Mu'nis al-Khadim raises his sword to kill Abullah ibn al-Mu'taz.

al-Muqtadir interrupts.

Al-Muqtadir:

Don't! Don't kill him.

Al-Sayyida:

Let him kill him.

Al-Muqtadir:

Take him to the prison, and let him rot there until he dies.

Mu'nis al-Khadim and Mu'nis al-Khazin leave while pulling Abdullah ibn al-Mu'taz who screams threateningly:

(To al-Sayyida) I will kill you with my own hands.

You all will die a terrible death when the Caliphacy returns to me.

(To al-Sayyida) You will die; and you all will, too.

Curtains close.

Act II

Place:

The Residence of Abu Sa'id al-Jannabi in Hajar.

Setting:

The *majlis* of Abu Sa'id al-Jannabi.

Seen in the majlis is Saqlabi, the private servant of Abu Sa'id al-Jannabi, and a junior servant.

Junior Servant:

Since I started serving in this house, I have never seen Abu Sa'id al-Jannabi pray or fast. But, you are a true Muslim. You taught me how to worship and recite the Qur'an. By Allah, I love you as a brother to me.

Saqlabi:

This man who calls himself "Master" is no one's master. Listen to me carefully …

(He takes him aside) and says:

His name is Hassan Bahram, originally a Persian miller from Jannabah. He was banished from there, and so he crossed the Gulf to Qatif where he became a flour merchant. There he started calling for supporters from among the Arabs to his Qaramatian *mazhab*. He gained many supporters and became the Chief of the Qaramatians and the main promoter of his *mazhab*. Caliph al-Mu'tadid went to war against him, but was defeated. As a result, Basra was sacked, the men were captured, the women and children taken as slaves. I was a soldier in the army of Caliph al-Mu'tadid but got captured by Hassan Bahram's men.

I am a free man, a free man … turned into a slave.

When they plundered Basra, they left nothing; the camels could not even lift the loot.

Junior Servant:

Where did all the looted money go?

Saqlabi:

He buried it all in the desert. The only one who knows its whereabouts is his younger son, Sulaiman.

Voices coming from the house entrance are heard.

The junior servant rushes to open the door. The voices get louder and closer.

Junior Servant *(to Saqlabi)*:

It is the Master. He is coming with the Commanders.

Both the Junior Servant and Saqlabi hide where they could eavesdrop.

Abu Sa'id:

What's the news from Baghdad?

A Commander:

All Baghdad's news is happy. Since al-Muqtadir became a Caliph six years ago, his relationship with the people there have suffered many ups and downs. Tremendously unsettled. One minute he is the Caliph, and another they remove him from office.

A Commander:

And the *vizirs* are busy competing in hunting Francolinus birds, and rewarding the hunters very handsomely.

A Commander:

It is very pleasing to know that they turned away from serious state affairs to complete indulgence in play and entertainment.

A Commander:

al-Muqtadir himself has no idea of the disastrous situation round him as his mother is not allowing any such news to reach his ears.

A Commander:

al-Mu'tadid, al-Muqtadir's father, had mobilized his armies against me when I took over Basra. But I defeated his armies and he had to stop the fighting and seek peace.

A Commander:

This is our chance to turn the tables against them. I say we attack Baghdad, end the Abbasid Caliphacy and instate the Qaramatian instead.

(Abu Sa'id al-Jannabi stands up together with the commanders. He walks towards one adjacent room) and says:

This requires careful planning.

(He ponders a little) then says:

Wait for me in the next room.

(Calling for the Junior Servant):

Boy! Come her, boy!
The Junior Servant rushes in.

Abu Sa'id al-Jannabi *(to the Junior Servant)*:

Lead the Commanders to the adjacent room and serve them well.

The Commanders leave with the Servant through the majlis door.

Abu Sa'id al-Jannabi *(calling the other servant)*:

Saqlabi! Saqlabi! Where are you, servant?

Saqlabi *(rushes out of his hideout)* **and says:**

Yes, Master!

Abu Sa'id:

Prepare the bath for me. I need to wash.

Abu Sa'id exits from the door he was standing by.

Saqlabi:

Immediately, Master!

Saqlabi stands in the middle of the majlis and whispers to himself in anger.

Saqlabi:

They want to attack Baghdad! Baghdad is my homeland! There, live my mother and father. Baghdad! That is where my wife and children are. It is where my brothers and sister live. Baghdad is where my mates, the Caliphate Soldiers, are. By Allah, I will not let you do it!

He then brings a big knife and waves it with his hand.

Saqlabi:

By Allah, I will not let you do it! ... I will kill you first.

(Saqlabi enters the bathroom. The sounds of the pouring of water and clunking of pots are heard. Then Saqlabi comes out with the knife in his hand).

Abu Sa'id al-Jannabi *(calling from his private room)*:

Servant! Is the bath ready?

Saqlabi (hides the knife in his waistband from behind. He receives Abu Sa'id al-Jannabi face to face).

Saqlabi:

The bath is ready, Master.

(Abu Sa'id heads for the bathroom. At the door, Saqlabi stabs him in the back. Abu Sa'id groans in pain and Saqlabi pushes him into the bathroom)

(Saqlabi heads to the middle of the majlis with the knife in his hand behind his back, and calls for a Commander)

Saqlabi:

Commander! Commander!

One of the Commanders comes in.

Saqlabi:

The Master wants to have a word with you.

Saqlabi directs the Commander to the bathroom door. When the Commander steps in, Saqlabi stabs him in the back. The Commander groans in pain and falls dead.
Saqlabi heads back to the middle of the majlis with the knife in his hand behind his back, and calls for another Commander)

Saqlabi:

Commander! Commander!

One of the Commanders comes in.

Saqlabi:

The Master wants to have a word with you.

Saqlabi directs the Commander to the bathroom door. When the Commander steps in, Saqlabi stabs him in the back. The Commander groans in pain and falls dead.
(Saqlabi heads back to the middle of the majlis with the knife in his hand behind his back, and calls for the third Commander)

Saqlabi:

Commander! Commander!

One of the Commanders comes in.

Saqlabi:

The Master wants to have a word with you.

Saqlabi directs the Commander to the bathroom door. When the Commander steps in, Saqlabi stabs him in the back. The Commander groans in pain and falls dead.
(Saqlabi heads back to the middle of the majlis with the knife in his hand behind his back, and calls for the fourth Commander)

Saqlabi:

Commander! Commander!

One of the Commanders comes in.

Saqlabi:

The Master wants to have a word with you.

Saqlabi directs the Commander to the bathroom door. When the Commander steps in, Saqlabi stabs him in the back. The Commander groans in pain and falls dead.
(Saqlabi heads back to the middle of the majlis with the knife in his hand behind his back, and calls for the fifth Commander)

Saqlabi:

Commander! Commander!

The fifth Commanders comes in.

Saqlabi:

The Master wants to have a word with you.

Saqlabi directs the Commander to the bathroom door. As he looks down at the floor, he sees bloodstains. He looks into the bathroom as he approaches it and sees the slaughtered bodies, one on top of the other. Saqlabi tries to attack the Commander and push him into the bathroom, but he was much stronger. A fight between them ensues and as they fight, the Commander loudly shouts:

Fifth Commander:

Sa'id! Sulaiman!

The servant has skilled your father.

Guards, the servant has killed your Master!

Everyone, the servant has killed the Commanders!

The guards and the courtiers come in. Saqlabi is caught and his hands are tied behind his back. His legs are tied, too. He is pushed to the ground in the middle of the majlis parallel to the audience. The dead bodies of the Commanders, covered in blood, are brought out and pulled to the middle of the majlis. Their heads face the audience. The two sons of Abu Sa'id arrive to the scene: Sa'id is the eldest and Sulaiman is the youngest of the two.

Sa'id and Sulaiman (bend over the body of their father, and scream):

Who did it? Who did it?

Fifth Commander:

The Saqlabi servant did it. He is here. Over here, Sa'id.

Sa'id ibn Abu Sa'id walks over eyeing Saqlabi. One of the guards raises his sword to kill Saqlabi, but Sa'id stops him, and shouts in anger:

Sa'id:

Bring me a pair of pincers ... now.

A man rushes to get the pincers.

Sa'id *(calling his brother):*

Brother Sulaiman! Abu Taher!

Sulaiman, Abu Taher:

Yes, Sa'id.

Sa'id:

Move my father's body together with the bodies of the Commanders to the side room.

A man comes in bringing the pincers, and gives them to Sa'id.

Sa'id *(to the guards)*:

Remove the clothes of the Saqlabi Servant.

Sa'id *(holding the pincers and addressing Saqlabi)*:

I will tear your body to pieces with these pincers.

Sa'id starts tearing the body with the pincers while he says:

Piece by piece. Piece by piece. Piece by piece.

The Saqlabi servant screams in agony. Sa'id continues while throwing each piece of flesh on the stage, right and left.

Sa'id :

Piece by piece. Piece by piece. Piece by piece.

Curtains close

The Black Stone

Act III

Scene 1

Setting:

An open court outside the house of Abu Taher Sulaiman ibn Abu Sa'id al-Jannabi. At the top of the house entrance door is a sign saying *"House of Hijra"*.

In the court, an old man with a turban sitting on a long wooden bench. He used to be the fifth commander who survived the attack when Abu Sa'id al-Jannabi was murdered many years back. Arrives another man with an Arabian headdress. He greets the commander.

The Arabian:

Peace be with you.

The Fifth Commander:

With you be Peace.

The Arabian:

Is this the house of Abu Taher Sulaiman al-Jannabi?

The Fifth Commander:

Who are you? And what do you want from Abu Taher?

The Arabian:

I am a Bedouin from the Arabian Desert. I came to join abu Taher's group. And you? Who are you?

The Fifth Commander:

Have you heard of the killing of Abu Sa'id al-Jannabi and his company of commanders in 301 AH?

The Arabian:

Yes, sure.

The Fifth Commander:

I was the one who survived that day.

The Arabian:

Ah! Then, you must be working for Abu Taher al-Jannabi. You can help me join his group.

The Fifth Commander:

Well, after Abu Sa'id al-Jannabi was killed, his son Sa'id became the Master. I was in his service for four years. Then, his younger brother, Abu Taher Sulaiman al-Jannabi, ousted him in 305 AH and took over, and cut us off as well.

The Arabian:

I see. Why are you here at his house today then?

The Fifth Commander:

I was told he would shortly be arriving from Mecca. So, I thought to myself if I come to receive him, he may feel sorry for the state I am in especially after his *hajj* journey, and may then provide me with some money I could live on.

The Arabian:

Yes, they say he has plenty of money.

The Fifth Commander:

True. After Abu Taher seized power 15 years ago, he used to take the people to the desert and say to them '*dig here and you will find money*'. They would and indeed find money. This was part of the money, which he and his father had hidden away, and no one knew anything about it. Every time, he would take the people to a different place and after digging the money out, he would keep most of it for himself and give them just a little. They foolishly believed that he had knowledge of the *Unseen*.

The Arabian:

How has he been like?

The Fifth Commander:

Well, since early 316 AH, he has been spreading corruption everywhere. He attacked Kufa, Rahba, Mosul and Singar, killed the inhabitants and seized they money and property.

His followers have also been in the increase. They continue to ransack the towns, kill the people, and loot their wealth. Now, when anyone hears about the Qaramatian, Abu Taher Sulaiman ibn Abu Sa'id al-Jannabi, they run away. Look what he did after his return from his looting expeditions ... He placed a sign above his entrance door saying *Dar al-Hijrah*. What a mockery!

The Arabian:

So, where is he now?

The Fifth Commander:

He went to Mecca for *hajj*. May Allah have mercy on the pilgrims there and save them from his wickedness!

Sounds of singing and Aarda music are heard approaching.
A man rushes in, shouting:

Man:

Abu Taher, the Qaramatian, has arrived.

Abu Taher, the Qaramatian, has arrived.

45

The Aarda band enters and dances while Abu Taher walks in carrying a basket in his hands.

Abu Taher:

Quiet! Quiet!

The dancing and singing stop.

Abu Taher:

Sit! Sit.

I went for *Hajj*; but I did not like it. So, I went out with my men on the day of *Tarwiyah*,[1] attacked the pilgrims and took their properties. We killed many of them, too. I then ordered the dead bodies to be thrown into the *Well of Zamzam*. I also ordered the *Kaabah* covers be removed and I tore them to pieces in front of my followers. Then, I removed the *Black Stone*. We took it out by force. The surviving pilgrims were screaming 'No, no'… and I kept saying 'Where are the *Ababil* swarms

---

1- Yawm al-Tarwiyah: This day falls on the 8th of Dhu-Hijjah, when the multitudes of pilgrims head for Mina for one of the major Hajj rituals.

of birds which would pelt us with hard stones that have our names carved on them? Where are they?

(Abu Taher opens his basket and takes out the Black Stone)

Abu Taher:

Here it is! Here is *The Black Stone*.

I brought it with me.

Here! Come! You all, walk round the basket with the stone in it.

Say with me:

I am Allah, and Allah is I.

I create at will and cause all to die.

The Aarda band resumes the drumming and singing, while repeating:

The Aarda:

He is Allah, and Allah is him!

He creates all, and causes death to them.

The singing continues while the curtains Close

Scene 2

Setting:

The open court before Dar al-Hijra of Abu Taher Sulaiman al-Jannabi. On the wooden bench, an old man is sitting. He is Muhammad Sanbar ibn al-Hassan ibn Sanbar.

Two men arrive; one looks like a merchant and the other is a local guide.

The Guide (pointing at Muhammad Sanbar ibn al-Hassan):

This is him. Muhammad Sanbar ibn al-Hassan.

The guide leaves, and the merchant greets Muhammad Sanbar who lets the man sit beside him.

Muhammad Sanbar:

Where are you from, stranger?

The Merchant:

I am a merchant from Isfahan. I came with my trade to Qatif. But when I heard about this man called *al-Zikri* who has taken the name 'Abul-Fadl Zakariyya', I decided to come to Hajar, to warn the people here against him. .. You may not know that he is the son of one of the Kings of Persia, from Isfahan. He had established there a headquarters for his deviant *call*.

Muhammad Sanbar:

If anyone in this town of Hajar were to hear you say this, you would be killed immediately.

Merchant, refrain from this talk here and mind only your trade.

In fact, it is better if you leave this town immediately. Hurry up and do not speak another word. Hurry up! Hurry up.

After a short while, a good-looking, lightly bearded young man with a beaming face walks in. He is dressed in a yellow garment, a matching turban and ties a band round his waist. Muhammad Sanbar greets the young man very humbly.

Muhammad Sanbar:

Welcome, Abul-Fadl Zakariyya! Please, please, come and sit.

Abul-Fadl Zakariyya:

When you visited my father, your friend, in Isfahan, you agreed with him to the killing of your opponent and competitor, Abu Hafs al-Sharik ibn Zarqan, who is Abu Taher's brother-in-law, in order that you become the only one on the scene. My father commissioned me to do so. But, you did not fulfil your promise of delivering power to me and making me 'the Master'.

Muhammad Sanbar:

I taught your father the secrets of Abu Sa'id al-Jannabi, and revealed to him the mysteries of the Qaramatians, their sciences and signals because I was a member of his innermost circle.

I promised to make your father a Master for all to obey, and no one would do anything without his permission.

Now, you come to take your father's place and act in mysterious ways!

What is it that you want by all this?

Abul-Fadl Zakariyya:

I want to kill Abu Taher, the Qaramatian, and become the Master of all Qaramatians.

Muhammad Sanbar:

Where are you going to find Abu Taher to kill him?

He is now in Rahbah, and will soon invade Ramla and seize Damascus. Do not rush to anything. I fear that your plan may be discovered.

Abul-Fadl Zakariyya:

There is no one who knows my plan except for you, is there?

Muhammad Sanbar:

There is talk in the town.

Abul-Fadl Zakariyya:

What do they say?

Muhammad Sanbar:

People say you are not a Muslim and that you are a son of a Persian King. They also say you established a centre in Isfahan for your *call*, which aims to overthrow the Islamic Caliphate in Baghdad.

Singing of army men is heard ... Abu Taher, the Qaramatian, arrives with his group. As soon as he sees Abul-Fadal Zakariyya, he points at him and shouts loudly:

Abu Taher, the Qaramatian:

This is my Lord and your Lord! This my God and your God!

(Abu Taher, the Qaramatian, raises Zakariyya on a high seat) and says:

We are all your obedient servants! The command is yours! You have power over us all.

Abu Taher and his men start picking dust and throwing it on their heads while repeating:

Our Lord! Our Lord. Our Lord!

Abu Taher:

Know all people that the *Proof* has come to being; it is nothing less than the religion of our father, Adam, himself. Any religion we belonged to before now is false. Everything the preachers had said is also false. Moses, Jesus and Muhammad, are all false. The true religion is that of Adam; the rest are all lying imposters. So, curse them all.

The group *(as they walk round the seat)*:

May they be cursed. May they be cursed. May they be cursed.

Abul-Fadl Zakariyya:

O, people! I decree that you no longer need to pray or fast. I make permissible sodomy, incest, and alcohol.

I command that in this town you establish four houses, one in each direction. These woul be dedicated to the worship of fire, which should be kept on day and night.

Then, Abu Taher together with his group start to take off their clothes, only leaving their private parts covered. They circumambulate Abul-Fadl Zakariyyah's seat, while chanting:

The group:

Our Lord, the Almighty;

Our Lord, full of Majesty;

Our Lord, the Almighty;

Our Lord, full of Majesty.

Curtains close

Act IV

Place:

House of Abu Sa'id al-Jannabi (as in the previous scene)

Knocking on the door. The servant goes then returns and says:

Servant:

Master! Master! Muhammad Sanbar is at the door requesting to see you.

Abu Taher, the Qaramatian:

Let him in.

Muhammad Sanbar enters looking shocked. He addresses Abu Taher.

Muhammad Sanbar:

What was that which you did yesterday, Abu Taher?

You caused your status and high esteem to diminish before everyone!

Abu Taher, the Qaramatian:

I was told that the Awaited *Mahadi* has appeared, and that he has had complete control over the people of Hajar. So, I rushed back from Rhaba and relinquished my plans to conquer Ramla and Damasus. As I arrived and saw him, I was so scared that he might turn me into a freak or a monster. The fear got the better of and, I acted that way only to appease him.

Muhammad Sanbar:

Did you know that Abul-Fadl Zakariyyah is not even a Muslim and that he is from Isfahan?

Abu Taher, the Qaramatian:

What? He's not a Muslim?

Muhammad Sanbar:

Did you not know that he is the one who killed your brother-in-law, Abu Hafs al-Sharik ibn Zarqan? He also killed your nephew, Hafs!

Abu Taher, the Qaramatian:

Wait! Wait! Hold on! Mother! Furjah! Um Sa'id! Come, come.

Furjah enters *(saying)*:
Yes, my son!

Abu Taher, the Qaramatian:

Come! Come and listen to what Muhammad Sanbar is saying. He says Abul-Fadl Zakariyyah is not a Muslim and that he killed you son-in-law, Abu Hafs al-Sharik ibn Zarqan, and your grandson, Hafs, too.

Furjah:

May Allah curse him.

Muhammad Sanbar (*addressing Abu Taher, the Qaramatian*)**:**

And he raped your sister!

Furjah (*screaming*)**:**

O, my Lord! What a disaster!

Abu Taher smacks his head with his hands and groans in pain.

Muhammad Sanbar (*addressing Abu Taher, the Qaramatian*)**:**

And now he is bent on killing you.

Abu Taher:

It will be I, who will kill him!

Muhammad Sanbar:

How are you going to kill him when he is

surrounded by his guards in the court outside your house?

Abu Taher:

We trick him to come in.

Muhammad Sanbar:

How?

Abu Taher *(pensively)*:

Yes, how? How?

He then turns to his mother and says:

Mother! I will trick this criminal to come in so that he may enter the house without his guards. When he is in, we'll kill him. Do not be scared, mother! Just calm down!

(Directing his speech to Muhammad Sanbar)

You go to him Muhammad Sanbar and say: 'Our Lord and Master! Furjah, Abu Taher's mother, has died. We would like you to come, open her up and fill her guts with charcoal as you had prescribed for us to do with the dead.'

I will make my mother lie here under the covers, pretending to be dead,

Muhammad Sanbar leaves. Abu Taher's sister enters.

Abu Taher's sister:

I heard everything.

Abu Taher (*angrily to his sister*):

Shame on you! Get out of my sight!

Furjah:

Please, do not scold her. She had been raped. She told me all about it.

Abu Taher (*addressing his mother*):

Here! Lie down. I will cover you. Do not move.

(*Furjah lies down on the floor. Abu Taher covers her with a sheet while the sister walks out, saying*):

Abu Taher's sister:

He must be killed. He must be killed. He must be killed.

(*The mother raises her head and says*):

He must be killed. He must be killed.

(*Abu Taher pushes her head down*).

Knocking on the door. Abu Taher opens the door. Abul-Fadl Zakariyya enters with Muhammad Sanbar. Abu Taher prostrates and addresses Abul-Fadl:

Abu Taher:

My Lord! My Lord!

Then he sobs and cries loudly.

Abu Taher:

My mother, Furjah, has died!

(Abul-Fadl Zakariyya takes a knife out of his pocket and bends over to cut Furjah open)

Abul-Fadl Zakariyya:

We cut her open and fill her guts with charcoal.
As he says this, Furjah's feet tremble.

(Abul-Fadl Zakariyya sees her movement and gets suspicious. Abu Taher holds Abul-Fadl Zakariyya's hand with the knife to stop him from cutting his mother open).

Abu Taher:

My Lord! Please, bring her back to life for me.

Abul-Fadl Zakariyya:

She is unworthy. She is a heretic. I will cut her open.

Furjah's feet tremble again of fear. Abul-Fadl looks at her. Abu Taher holds Abul-Fadl's hand and says:

Abu Taher:

No, no. Please, my Lord. Bring her back to life.

(Abul-Fadl Zakariyya bends over Furjah again with the knife while making some unusal sorcerer's moves and gestures)

Abul-Fadl Zakariyya:

I will cut her belly open.

Furjah's feet move again.

Abu Taher *(holding Abul-Fadl's hand)*:

No, no. My Lord. Please, bring her back to life.

Abul-Fadl Zakariyya *(realizing it was all part of a plot against him)*:

Do not rush me. The power to raise the dead had been taken away from me. Wait until my father is here and he will bring her back to life.

(Abu Sa'id ibn Hassan al-Jannabi enters in a hurry with a knife in his hand. He holds Abul-Fadl from behind and puts the knife agaist his throat).

Abul-Fadl Zakariyya *(screaming in fear)*:

Please, do not kill me. I do not want to be a Master. I will be your servant. I will look after your sheep and cattle! Do not kill me.

Abu Taher:

No, no, Sa'id.

Sa'id:

My sister told me everything.

Abul-Fadl Zakariyya (*screaming*):

Guards! Guards!

Sa'id slits the throat of Abul-Fadl Zakariyya whose blood flows on the ground and he drops dead.

Loud knocking on the door with voices shouting:
Open the door! (*Knocking*) Open the door!

Muhammad Sanbar:

It's the gurads. Abul Fadl's guards.

Abu Taher (*addressing Muhammad Sanbar*):

Throw them some money! Hurry!

The sister:

Cut his tummy open and pull his liver out. Let me chew on it!

(Sa'id cuts Abul-Fadl Zakariyya open. Abu Taher and Muhammad Sanbar throw money from the window to keep the guards outside busy. They repeat:

Throw them money. Silence them with money. Throw them money. Silence them with money.

Curtains close

Act V

Setting:

An open arena representing the Meccan Holy House Tawaf area.[1]

Time:

5th Dul-Hijjah, 339 AH (corresponding to 15th May, 951 CE).

Sounds of prayers and supplications to Allah are filling the place.

Labbayaka Allahumma Labbayk.

Labbayaka la Sharika laka Labbayk.

O, Allah, here we are, responding to Your Call.

O, Allah, You have no partner.

Praise be to you. All the blessings and dominion belong to you.

Your have no pratners.

1- Tawaf is the circumambulation of the Kaabah by the pilgrims and visitors.

The prayers continue. A man climbs up the pulpit and announces:

The Governor of Mecca would like to address you all.

He climbs down, and the Governor of Mecca goes up.

Governor of Mecca:

O, Muslims! O, Muslims!

His voice can hardly be heard with the sounds of the prayers of the multitudes of pilgrims.

Governor of Mecca:

O, Muslims! O, Muslims!

The pilgrims listen.

Governor of Mecca:

O, pilgrims. Visitors of Allah's Sacred House! You should be joyous this year of 339 AH. You should be joyous, as today the *Black Stone* has been restored after being stolen and kept away for twenty-two years.

O, Muslims! Visitors of Allah's Holy Sanctuary! With us today is Muhammad Sanbar ibn al-Hassan ibn Muhammad Sanbar. He is the one who retrieved the *Black Stone*. Before we put it back in its original place, I would like to say the following:

O, Muslims! Unite under the banner of *'There is no god but Allah. Muhammad is the Messenger of Allah'*.

O, Muslims! Stay clear from the hypocrites who pretend to be your friends!

O, Muslims! Purify your hearts and remove all malice from your souls!

O, Muslims! Love one another in Allah. Love one another in Allah.

Now, let Muhammad Sanbar come over here. Let him climb up the pulpit to show you the *Black Stone* himself. We will then return it to its original place where it belongs.

Muhammad Sanbar goes up the pulpit and opens the basket. He picks up the Black Stone and shows it to the people. The pilgrims raise their voices with prayers and supplications, saying:

Allahu Akbar. Allah is great. Allah is great.

There is no god but Allah.

Allahu Akbar. Allahu Akbar. Praise be to Allah.

The prayers continue.

Muhammad Sanbar comes down and heads with the Governor of Mecca towards the corner of the

Kaabah where the Black Stone should be placed. The prayers continue.

The actors come in one after the other. They all share in the *Tawaf* round the Kaabah. Some kiss the *Black Stine*. They are all chanting the prayers repeatedly. They head towards the audience chanting '*Allahu Akbar*' and urge them to participate in the chanting. The Chanting and prayers continue.

The End

www.ingramcontent.com/pod-product-compliance
Lightning Source LLC
Chambersburg PA
CBHW070555160726
48003CB00005B/2061